WORLD CUP

2019

REVIEW

By Wayne Grobler

CONTENTS

4. Match 1

44. Final Pool Standings

55. The Final

67. Tournament Stats

77. Team by Team Results

PROLOGUE

This handbook contains all the match statistics for every one of the 48 matches played in the 2019 World Cup, rugby's global showpiece event.

The tournament was hosted by Japan, the first for an Asian nation. Having shocked South Africa in the 2015 tournament the Japanese were ready to take a step up in the 2019 edition.

The Japanese people were excellent hosts and hosted a successful event. Never before had a host nation done so much to welcome visiting fans and it ensured that the tournament would go down in history as one of the best ever.

The Japanese team rose to the occasion and added two more shock results as they defeated both Ireland and Scotland on their way to an unbeaten run through the pool stages.

In the following pages all the match statistics are recorded as we look back at a truly memorable tournament.

MATCH 1

Friday 20 September 2019

Tokyo Stadium, Tokyo

Referee : Nigel Owens

JAPAN 30

Tries : Katoro Matsushima (3)

       Pieter Labuschagne

Conversions : Yu Tamura

          Rikiya Matsuda

Penalties : Yu Tamura (2)

RUSSIA 10

Try : Kirill Golosnitsky

Conversion : Yury Kushnarev

Penalty : Yury Kushnarev

Player of the match : Kotaro Matsushima

MATCH 2

Saturday 21 September 2019

Sapporo Dome, Sapporo

Referee : Ben O' Keeffe

AUSTRALIA 39

Tries : Tolu Latu (2), Michael Hooper, Reece Hodge, Samu Kerevi, Marika Koroibete

Conversions : Christian Lealilifano, Matt Toomua (2)

Penalty : Reece Hodge

FIJI 21

Tries : Peceli Yato, Waisea Nayacadevu

Conversion : Ben Volavola

Penalties : Ben Volavola (3)

Player of the match : Tolu Latu

MATCH 3

Saturday 21 September 2019

Tokyo Stadium, Tokyo

Referee : Angus Gardner

FRANCE   23

Tries : Gael Fickou, Antoine Dupont

Conversions : Romain Ntamack (2)

Penalties : Romain Ntamack (2)

Drop Goal : Camille Lopez

ARGENTINA   21

Tries : Guido Petti, Julian Montoya

Conversion : Nicolas Sanchez

Penalties : Benjamin Urdapiletta (2), Nicolas Sanchez

Player of the match : Gael Fickou

MATCH 4

Saturday 21 September 2019

International Stadium, Yokohama City

Referee : Jerome Garces

NEW ZEALAND   23

Tries : George Bridge, Scott Barrett

Conversions : Richie Mo'unga (2)

Penalties : Richie Mo'unga (2), Beauden Barrett

SOUTH AFRICA   13

Tries : Pieter Steph du Toit

Conversion : Handre Pollard

Penalty : Handre Pollard

Drop Goal : Handre Pollard

Player of the match : Beauden Barrett

8

MATCH 5

Sunday 22 September 2019

Hanazono Rugby Stadium, Higashiosaka City

Referee : Nic Berry

ITALY   47

Tries : Tommaso Allen, Tilo Tebaldi, Mattia Bellini, Carlo Canna, Penalty Try , Jake Polledi, Mateo Minozzi

Conversions : Tomasso Allen (3), Carlo Canna (2)

NAMIBIA   22

Tries : Damian Stevens, JC Greyling, Chad Plato

Conversions : Cliven Loubser (2)

Penalty : Cliven Loubser

Player of the match : Federico Ruzza

MATCH 6

Sunday 22 September 2019

International Stadium Yokohama City

Referee : Wayne Barnes

IRELAND   27

Tries : James Ryan, Rory Best,

      Tadgh Furlong, Andrew Conway

Conversions : Johnny Sexton, Conor Murray

Penalty : Jack Carty

SCOTLAND   3

Penalty : Greg Laidlaw

Player of the match : CJ Stander

MATCH 7

Sunday 22 September 2019

Sapporo Dome, Sapporo

Referee : Paul Williams

ENGLAND   35

Tries : Manu Tuilagi (2),

       Jamie George

       Luke Cowan Dickie

Conversions : Owen Farrell (3)

Penalties : Owen Farrell (3)

TONGA   3

Penalty : Sonatane Takulia

Player of the match : Manu Tuilagi

MATCH 8

Monday 23 September 2019

City of Toyota Stadium, Toyota City

Referee : Luke Pearce

WALES   43

Tries : Jonathan Davies, Justin Tipuric, Josh Adams, Liam Williams, Tomos Williams, George North

Conversions : Dan Biggar (4), Leigh Halfpenny

Penalty : Dan Biggar

GEORGIA   14

Tries : Shalva Mamukashvili, Levan Chilachava

Conversions : Tedo Abzhandadze (2)

Player of the match : Jake Ball

MATCH 9

Tuesday 24 September 2019

Kumagaya Rugby Stadium, Kumagaya City

Referee : Romain Poite

SAMOA   34

Tries : Alapati Leiua (2), Ed Fidow (2),
   Afaesetiti Amosa, Rey Lee – Lo

Conversions : Tusi Pisi (2)

RUSSIA   9

Penalties : Yury Kushnarev (2)

Drop Goal : Yury Kushnarev

Player of the match : Alapati Leiua

MATCH 10

Wednesday 25 September 2019

Kamaishi Recovery Memorial Stadium, Kamaishi City

Referee : Pascal Gauzere

URUGUAY   30

Tries : Santiago Arata, Manuel Diana, Juan Manuel Cat

Conversions : Felipe Berchesi (3)

Penalties : Felipe Berchesi (3)

FIJI   27

Tries : Mosulame Dolokoto, Erani Mawa, Api Ratuniyarawa, Nikola Matawalu (2)

Conversion : Josh Matavesi

Player of the match : Felipi Berschesi

MATCH 11

Thursday 26 September 2019

Fukuoka Hakatanomori Stadium, Fukuoka City

Referee : Nigel Owens

ITALY   48

Tries : Braam Steyn, Dean Budd, Sebastian Negri, Mattia Bellini, Federico Zani, Matteo Minozzi, Penalty Try

Conversions : Tommaso Allen (3), Carlo Canna

Penalties : Tommaso Allen (2)

CANADA   7

Try : Andrew Coe

Conversion : Peter Nelson

Player of the match : Jake Polledri

MATCH 12

Thursday 26 September 2019

Kobe Misaki Stadium, Kobe City

Referee : Nic Berry

ENGLAND   45

Tries : Joe Cokanasiga (2), George Ford, Billy Vunipola, Luke Cowan Dickie, Ruaridh McConnochie, Lewis Ludlam

Conversions : George Ford (5)

UNITED STATES   7

Try : Bryce Campbell

Conversion : AJ MacGinty

Player of the Match : George Ford

MATCH 13

Saturday 28 September 2019

Hanazone Rugby Stadium, Higashiosaka City

Referee : Jaco Peyper

ARGENTINA   28

Tries : Julian Montoya (3), Santiago Carreras

Conversions : Benjamin Urdapilleta (4)

TONGA   12

Tries : Telusa Veainu (2)

Conversion : Sonatone Takulua

Player of the match : Julian Montoya

MATCH 14

Saturday 28 September 2019

Shizuoka Stadium, Shizuoka

Referee : Angus Gardner

JAPAN   19

Try : Kenki Fukuoka

Conversion : Yu Tamura

Penalties : Yu Tamura (4)

IRELAND   12

Tries : Garry Ringrose, Rob Kearney

Conversion : Jack Carty

Player of the match : Shota Horie

MATCH 15

Saturday 28 September 2019

City of Toyota Stadium, Toyota City

Referee : Mathieu Raynal

SOUTH AFRICA 57

Tries : Bongi Mbonambi (2), Makazole Mapimpi (2), Francois Louw, Lukhanyo Am, Warrick Gelant, Siya Kolisi, Schalk Brits

Conversions : Elton Jantjies (6)

NAMIBIA 3

Penalty : Cliven Loubser

Player of the match : Lood de Jager

19

MATCH 16

Sunday 29 September 2019

Kumagaya Rugby Stadium, Kumagaya City

Referee : Wayne Barnes

GEORGIA   33

Tries : Alexander Todua, Otari Giorgadzo,

    Levan Chilacheva, Jaba Bregvadze,

    Giorgi Kveseladze

Conversions : Tedo Abzhandadze (4)

URUGUAY   7

Try : Andres Vilaseca

Conversion : Felipe Berchesi

Player of the match : Otari Giorgadze

20

MATCH 17

Sunday 29 September 2019

Tokyo Stadium, Tokyo

Referee : Romain Poite

WALES   29

Tries : Hadleigh Parkes, Gareth Davies

Conversions : Dan Biggar, Rhys Patchell

Penalties : Rhys Patchell (3)

Drop Goals : Dan Biggar, Rhys Patchell

AUSTRALIA   25

Tries : Adam Ashley – Cooper, Dane Haylett – Petty, Michael Hooper

Conversions : Matt Toomua (2)

Penalties : Bernard Foley, Matt Tooumua

Player of the match : Gareth Davies

MATCH 18

Monday 30 September 2019

Kobe Misaki Stadium, Kobe City

Referee : Pascal Gauzere

SCOTLAND   34

Tries : Sean Maitland ,

　　　　Greig Laidlaw,

　　　　Penalty Tries (2)

Conversions : Greig Laidlaw (2)

Penalty : Greig Laidlaw

Drop Goal : Stuart Hogg

SAMOA   0

Player of the match : Jonny Gray

MATCH 19

Wednesday 2 October 2019

Fukuoka Hakatonomari Stadium, Fukuoka City

Referee ; Ben O' Keeffe

FRANCE   33

Tries : Yoann Huget

　　　Aliveret Raka

　　　Baptiste Serin

　　　Gael Fickou

　　　Jefferson Poirot

Conversions : Camille Lopez (4)

UNITED STATES   9

Penalties : AJ MacGinty (3)

Player of the match : Camille Lopez

MATCH 20

Wednesday 2 October 2019

Oita Stadium, Oita

Referee : Romain Poite

NEW ZEALAND   63

Tries : Brad Weber (2), Jordie Barrett,

Sonny Bill Williams, Beauden Barrett,

Rieko Ioane, Scott Barrett,

Shannon Frizell, Penalty Try

Conversions : Richie Mo'unga (8)

CANADA   0

Player of the match : Richie Mo'unga

MATCH 21

Thursday 3 October 2019

Hanazono Rugby Stadium, Higashiosaka City

Referee : Paul Williams

FIJI   45

Tries : Waisea Nayacalevu, Frank Lomani, Josua Tuisava, Semi Radradra (2), Semi Kunatani, Api Ratuniyarawa

Conversions : Ben Volavola (5)

GEORGIA   10

Try : Mamuka Gorgodze

Conversion : Soso Matiashvili

Penalty : Soso Matiashvili

Player of the match : Semi Radradra

25

MATCH 22

Thursday 3 October 2019

Kobe Misaki Stadium, Kobe City

Referee : Jerome Garces

IRELAND   35

Tries : Rob Kearney

Peter O' Mahony

Rhys Ruddock

Andrew Conway

Garry Ringrose

Conversions : Johnny Sexton (3)

Jack Carty (2)

RUSSIA   0

Player of the match : Rhys Ruddock

MATCH 23

Friday 4 October 2019

Shizuoka Stadium, Shizuoka

Referee : Wayne Barnes

SOUTH AFRICA   49

Tries : Cheslin Kolbe (2) , Bongi Mbonambi

　　　　Lukhanyo Am

　　　　Makazole Mapimpi

　　　　RG Snyman

　　　　Malcolm Marx

Conversions : Handre Pollard (4)

Penalties : Handre Pollard (2)

ITALY   3

Penalty : Tommaso Allan

Player of the match : Cheslin Kolbe

MATCH 24

Saturday 5 October 2019

Oita Stadium, Oita

Referee : Mathieu Raynal

AUSTRALIA   45

Tries : Dane Haylett – Petty (2)

　　　　Jordan Petaia

　　　　Tevita Kuridrani (2)

　　　　Will Genia , James Slipper

Conversions : Christian Lealiifano (5)

URUGUAY   10

Try : Manuel Diana

Conversion : Felipe Berchesi

Penalty : Felipe Berchesi

Player of the match : Tevita Kuridrani

MATCH 25

Saturday 5 October 2019

Tokyo Stadium, Tokyo

Referee : Nigel Owens

ENGLAND   39

Tries : Jonny May, Elliot Daly, Ben Youngs

   George Ford , Jack Nowell

   Luke Cowan – Dickie

Conversions : Owen Farrell (3)

Penalty : Owen Farrell

ARGENTINA   10

Try : Matias Moroni

Conversion : Emiliano Boffelli

Penalty : Benjamin Urdapilleta

Player of the match : Sam Underhill

MATCH 26

Saturday 5 October 2019

City of Toyota Stadium, Toyota

Referee : Jaco Peyper

JAPAN   38

Tries : Timothy Lafaele, Kazuki Himeno,

　　　　Kenki Fukuoka, Kotaro Matsushima

Conversions : Yu Tamura (3)

Penalties : Yu Tamura (4)

SAMOA   19

Try : Henry Taefu

Conversion : Henry Taefu

Penalties : Henry Taefu (4)

Player of the match : Lomani Lemeki

MATCH 27

Sunday 6 October

Tokyo Stadium, Tokyo

Referee : Pascal Gauzere

NEW ZEALAND   71

Tries : Sevu Reece (2), Anton Lienert – Brown (2), Angus Ta'avdo, Ben Smith (2), Joe Moody, Sam Whitelock, Jordie Barrett, TJ Perenara

Conversions : Jordie Barrett (8)

NAMIBIA   9

Penalties : Damian Stevens (3)

Player of the match : Anton Lienert – Brown

MATCH 28

Sunday 6 October 2019

Kumamoto Stadium, Kumamoto City

Referee : Nic Berry

FRANCE   23

Tries : Virimi Vakatawa

   Alivereti Raka

Conversions : Romain Ntamack (2)

Penalties : Romain Ntamack (3)

TONGA   21

Tries : Sonatone Takulua

   Malietoa Hingano , Zane Kapeli

Conversions : Sonatone Takulua (2)

      Latiume Fosita (1)

Player of the match : Alivereti Raka

MATCH 29

Tuesday 8 October 2019

Kobe Misaki Stadium, Kobe City

Referee : Luke Pearce

SOUTH AFRICA   66

Tries : Cobus Reinach (3), Damian de Allende,
Sibusiso Nkosi, Warrick Gelant,
Frans Steyn, Schalk Brits,
Frans Malherbe

Conversions : Elton Jantjies (8)

CANADA   7

Try : Matt Heaton

Conversion : Peter Nelson

Player of the match : RG Snyman

MATCH 30

Wednesday 9 October 2019

Kumagaya Rugby Stadium, Kumagaya City

Referee : Paul Williams

ARGENTINA   47

Tries : Joaquin Tuculet (2), Nicolas Sanchez,

Juan Cruz Mallia (2), Gonzalo Bertanou,

Jeronimo DE La Fuenta

Conversions : Nicolas Sanchez (5)

Benjamin Urdapilleta

UNITED STATES   17

Tries : Blaine Scully (2)

Paul Lasike

Conversion : AJ MacGinty

Player of the match : Juan Cruz Mallia

MATCH 31

Wednesday 9 October 2019

Shizuoka Stadium, Shizuoka

Referee : Wayne Barnes

SCOTLAND   61

Tries : George Horne (3)

Adam Hastings (2)

George Turner

Tommy Seymour

John Barclay

Stuart McInally

Conversions : Adam Hastings (8)

RUSSIA   0

Player of the match : Adam Hastings

MATCH 32

Wednesday 9 October 2019

Oita Stadium, Oita

Referee : Jerome Garces

WALES   29

Tries : Josh Adams (3)

      Liam Williams

Conversions : Dan Biggar (2)

      Rhys Patchell

Penalty: Rhys Patchell

FIJI   17

Tries : Josua Tuisova

      Kini Murimurivalu

      Penalty Try

Player of the match : Semi Radradra

MATCH 33

Friday 11 October 2019

Shizuoka Stadium, Shizuoka

Referee : Pascal Gauzere

AUSTRALIA   27

Tries : Nic White

      Marika Koroibete

      Jack Dempsey

      Will Genia

Conversions : Matt Toomua (2)

Penalty : Matt Toomua

GEORGIA   8

Try : Alexander Todua

Penalty : Soso Matiashvili

Player of the match : Izack Rodda

MATCH 34

Saturday 12 October 2019

NEW ZEALAND 0

ITALY 0

Due to Typhoon Hagibis the match was cancelled and both teams were awarded 2 points each. New Zealand topped pool A in any event and progressed to the quarter final. Italy did not qualify to progress.

MATCH 35

Saturday 12 October 2019

ENGLAND 0

FRANCE 0

Due to Typhoon Hagabis the match was cancelled and both teams were awarded 2 points. Both teams progressed to the quarter finals.

MATCH 36

Saturday 12 October 2019

Fukuoka Hakatano Stadium, Fukuoka Stadium

Referee : Nic Berry

IRELAND   47

Tries : Jonny Sexton (2) , Rory Best

　　　　Tadhg Furlong

　　　　Jordan Larmour

　　　　CJ Stander

　　　　Andrew Conway

Conversions : Jonny Sexton (4)

　　　　　　　Joey Carberry (2)

SAMOA   5

Try : Jack Lam

Player of the match : Jordan Larmour

MATCH 37

Sunday 13 October

NAMIBIA 0

CANADA 0

Due to Typhoon Hagabis the match was cancelled and both teams were awarded 2 points. Both teams failed to progress and would have targeted the match as their only chance for victory.

MATCH 38

Sunday 13 October 2019

Hanazano Rugby Stadium, Higashiosaka City

Referee : Nigel Owens

TONGA   31

Tries : Siegfried Fisiihoi , Malietoa Hingano

Siale Piutau

Telusa Veainu

Conversions : Sonatone Takulua (2)

James Faiva, Siale Piutau

UNITED STATES   19

Tries : Mike Teo (2)

Tony Lamborn

Conversions : AJ MacGinty (2)

Player of the match : Siale Piutau

MATCH 39

Sunday 13 October 2019

Kumamoto Stadium, Kumamoto City

Referee : Angus Gardner

WALES   35

Tries : Nicky Smith , Josh Adams

　　　　Tomas Williams

　　　　Gareth Davies

　　　　Penalty Try

Conversions : Leigh Halfpenny (4)

URUGUAY   13

Try : German Kessler

Conversion : Felipe Berchesi

Penalties : Felipe Berchesi (2)

Player of the match : Leigh Halfpenny

43

MATCH 40

Sunday 13 October 2019

International Stadium Yokohama, Yokohama City

Referee : Ben O'Keefe

JAPAN   28

Tries : Kenki Fukuoka (2) , Kotaro Matsushima

Keita Inagaki

Conversions : Yu Tamura (4)

SCOTLAND   21

Tries : Finn Russell

Willem Nel

Zander Fagerson

Conversions : Greig Laidlaw (2)

Finn Russell

Player of the match : Kenki Fukuoka

FINAL POOL STANDINGS

POOL A

JAPAN

P : 4 W : 4 L : 0 D : 0 BP : 3 POINTS : 19

IRELAND

P : 4 W : 3 L : 1 D : 0 BP : 4 POINTS : 16

SCOTLAND

P : 4 W: 2 L : 2 D : 0 BP : 3 POINTS : 11

SAMOA

P : 4 W : 1 L : 3 D : 0 BP : 1 POINTS : 5

RUSSIA

P : 4 W : 0 L : 4 D : 0 BP : O POINTS : 0

POOL B

NEW ZEALAND

P : 4 W : 3 L : 0 D : 1 BP : 2 POINTS : 16

SOUTH AFRICA

P : 4 W : 3 L : 1 D : 0 BP : 3 POINTS : 15

ITALY

P : 4 W : 2 L : 1 D : 1 BP : 2 POINTS : 12

NAMIBIA

P : 4 W : 0 L : 3 D : 1 BP : 0 POINTS : 2

CANADA

P : 4 W : 0 L : 3 D : 1 BP : 0 POINTS : 2

POOL C

ENGLAND

P : 4 W : 3 L : 0 D : 1 BP : 3 POINTS : 17

FRANCE

P : 4 W : 3 L : 0 D : 1 BP : 1 POINTS : 15

ARGENTINA

P : 4 W : 2 L : 2 D : 0 BP : 3 POINTS : 11

TONGA

P : 4 W : 1 L : 3 D : 0 BP : 2 POINTS : 6

UNITED STATES

P : 4 W : 0 L : 4 D : 0 BP : 0 POINTS : 0

POOL D

WALES

P : 4 W : 4 L : 0 D : 0 BP : 3 POINTS : 19

AUSTRALIA

P : 4 W : 3 L : 1 D : 0 BP : 4 POINTS : 16

FIJI

P : 4 W : 1 L : 3 D : 0 BP : 3 POINTS : 7

GEORGIA

P : 4 W : 1 L : 3 D : 0 BP : 1 POINTS : 5

URUGUAY

P : 4 W : 1 L : 3 D : 0 BP : 0 POINTS : 4

MATCH 41   QUARTER FINAL 1

Saturday 19 October 2019

Oita Stadium, Oita

Referee : Jerome Garces

ENGLAND   40

Tries : Jonny May (2)

Kyle Sinckler

Anthony Watson

Conversions : Owen Farrell (4)

Penalties : Owen Farrell (4)

AUSTRALIA   16

Try : Marika Koroibete

Conversion : Christian Lealiifano

Penalties : Christian Lealiifano (3)

Player of the match : Tom Curry

MATCH 42   QUARTER FINAL 2

Saturday 19 October 2019

Tokyo Stadium, Tokyo

Referee : Nigel Owens

NEW ZEALAND   46

Tries : Aaron Smith (2), Beauden Barrett,

　　　　Codie Taylor, Matt Todd,

　　　　George Bridge, Jordie Barrett

Conversions : Richie Mo'unga (4)

Penalty : Richie Mo'unga

IRELAND   14

Tries : Robbie Henshaw, Penalty Try

Conversion : Joey Carbery

Player of the match : Beauden Barrett

MATCH 43   QUARTER FINAL 3

Sunday 20 October 2019

Oita Stadium, Oita

Referee : Jaco Peyper

WALES   20

Tries : Aaron Wainwright, Ross Moriarty

Conversions : Dan Biggar (2)

Penalties : Dan Biggar (2)

FRANCE   19

Tries : Sebastien Vahaamahina

　　　　Charles Ollivan

　　　　Virimi Vakatawa

Conversions : Romain Ntamack (2)

Player of the match : Aaron Wainwright

MATCH 44   QUARTER FINAL 4

Sunday 20 October 2019

Tokyo Stadium, Tokyo

Referee : Wayne Barnes

SOUTH AFRICA   26

Tries : Makazole Mapimpi (2)

      Faf de Klerk

Conversion : Handre Pollard

Penalties : Handre Pollard (3)

JAPAN   3

Penalty : Yu Tamura

Player of the match : Faf de Klerk

MATCH 45   SEMI FINAL 1

Saturday 26 October 2019

International Stadium, Yokohama City

Referee : Nigel Owens

ENGLAND   19

Tries : Manu Tuilagi

Conversion : Owen Farrell

Penalties : George Ford (4)

NEW ZEALAND   7

Try : Ardie Savea

Conversion : Richie Mo'unga

Player of the match : Maro Itoje

MATCH 46   SEMI FINAL 2

Sunday 27 October 2019

International Stadium, Yokohama City

Referee : Jerome Garces

SOUTH AFRICA   19

Try : Damian de Allende

Conversion : Handre Pollard

Penalties : Handre Pollard (4)

WALES   16

Try : Josh Adams

Conversion : Leigh Halfpenny

Penalties : Dan Biggar (3)

Player of the match : Handre Pollard

MATCH 47   THIRD PLACE PLAY OFF

Friday 1 November 2019

Referee: Wayne Barnes

NEW ZEALAND   40

Tries : Ben Smith (2), Joe Moody,
Beauden Barrett, Ryan Crotty,
Richie Mo'unga

Conversions : Richie Mo'unga (5)

WALES   17

Tries : Hallam Amos, Josh Adams

Conversions : Rhys Patchell
Dan Biggar

Penalty : Rhys Patchell

Player of the match : Brodie Retallick

THE FINAL

ENGLAND

- 15 Elliot Daly
- 11 Jonny May
- 12 Owen Farrell (c)
- 13 Manu Tuilagi
- 14 Anthony Watson
- 10 George Ford
- 9 Ben Youngs
- 1 Mako Vunipola
- 2 Jamie George
- 3 Kyle Sinckler
- 4 Maro Itoje
- 5 Courtney Lawes
- 6 Tom Curry
- 7 Sam Underhill

57

8   Billy Vunipola

ENGLAND RESERVES

16   Luke Cowan - Dickie

17   Joe Marler

18   Dan Cole

19   George Kruis

20   Mark Wilson

21   Ben Spencer

22   Henry Slade

23   Jonathan Joseph

COACH

Eddie Jones

Eddie Jones coached Australia to the final in 2003 where they lost to an extra time drop goal by Johnny Wilkinson.

SOUTH AFRICA

15 Willie Le Roux

11 Makazole Mapimpi

12 Damian de Allende

13 Lukhanyo Am

14 Cheslin Kolbe

10 Handre Pollard

9 Faf de Klerk

1 Tendai Mtawarira

2 Bongi Mbonambi

3 Frans Malherbe

4 Eben Etzebeth

5 Lood de Jager

6 Siya Kolisi (c)

7 Pieter – Steph du Toit

8 Duane Vermeulen

SOUTH AFRICA RESERVES

16 Malcolm Marx

17 Steven Kitshoff

18 Vincent Koch

19 RG Snyman

20 Franco Mostert

21 Francois Louw

22 Herschel Jantjies

23 Francois Steyn

COACH

Rassie Erasmus

Rassie was capped 36 times for South Africa and played in the 1999 tournament. He also captained South Africa in a test match.

REFEREE

JEROME GARCES

Nigel Owens injured himself during the first semi final and could therefore not be considered. Garces was a surprise appointment and upon being appointed he announced that the final would be his last test match before retiring.

Garces was appearing in his 56th and last test match in the final. He was the first Frenchman to referee a final.

VENUE

INTERNATIONAL STADIUM YOKOHAMA

The stadium was opened in March 1998 and has a capacity of 75, 000. It hosted seven matches during the tournament. Four of those were pool matches and includes the match between England and France that was cancelled due to Typhoon Hagibis.

It also hosted both the semi – final matches before hosting the final on the 2nd of November 2019.

FINAL SCORE

SOUTH AFRICA   32

ENGLAND   12

South Africa

Tries : Makazole Mapimpi

      Cheslin Kolbe

Conversions : Handre Pollard (2)

Penalties : Handre Pollard (6)

England

Penalties : Owen Farrell (4)

MATCH ANALYSIS

England were considered the favourites heading into the match, due to their comprehensive victory over the All Blacks in the semi final. South Africa struggled to beat Wales although their defence in that match was above par as has been the case the entire tournament.

South Africa was given an opportunity to put the first points on the board after two minutes but Pollard missed a kick he would have expected to slot. England prop Kyle Sinckler managed to knock himself out cold after a couple of minutes play as he attempted a tackle only to dive into the elbow of team mate Maro Itoje.

Dan Cole came on as substitute and was unable to handle the veteran Tendai Mtawarira. The Boks dominated the scrums, the line outs and just about every other facet of play. The English made silly mistakes and seemed unable to cope with the pressure.

Midway through the first half they attacked the Springbok try line but wave after wave of players were tackled back. There was simply no way through the defensive line of the South Africans.

Pollard kept the scoreboard ticking over and by half time the Boks were leading 12 – 6. The Boks turned the screws in the second half and eventually the pressure told as Makazole Mapimpi scored the first try of the match after some slick hand work from Lukhanyo Am.

It was also the first try South Africa has scored in a final. In the 73rd minute Am scooped up a loose ball to Pieter Steph du Toit who in turn passed to Cheslin Kolbe. Kolbe had some work to do but managed to step Owen Farrell and accelerate to the try line to seal the win beyond any doubt.

Pollard and converted and the score was 32 – 12. The Boks were on the attack again when the hooter went and Pollard kicked the ball out as victory was secured. Even the most biased Springbok supporter would not have predicted that the match would be won by such a handsome margin. But the South African coach Rassie Erasmus had a few tricks up his sleeve and obviously planned well.

When Frans Steyn took the field for South Africa late in the match he became the second South African, Os du Randt being the other, to win the tournament on two separate occasions. He played at centre in the 2007 final and this was his 67th test match in total.

Bok captain Siya Kolisi was appearing in his 50th test match and made it one to remember. It was South Africa's third title after their 1995 and 2007 victories.

PLAYER OF THE MATCH

DUANE VERMEULEN

Vermeulen was playing in his 54th test match. The burly number eight was massive in defence as usual and there were no complaints after he was named player of the match.

Vermeulen made his test debut in 2012 and earlier in 2019 he was handed the captaincy of the Springboks for the first time. He captained them twice during the season.

TOURNAMENT STATS

MOST POINTS

69 HANDRE POLLARD

58 OWEN FARRELL

54 RICHIE MO'UNGA

51 YU TAMURA

41 DAN BIGGAR

MOST TRIES

7 JOSH ADAMS

6 MAKAZOLE MAPIMPI

5 KOTARO MATSUSHIMA

4 BEN SMITH

4 JULIAN MONTOYA

DROP GOALS

CAMILLE LOPEZ

DAN BIGGAR

HANDRE POLLARD

RHYS PATCHELL

STUART HOGG

YURY KUSHNAREV

All the above players scored one drop goal each.

PENALTIES

16   HANDRE POLLARD

12   OWEN FARRELL

11   YU TAMURA

6   DAN BIGGAR

6   FELIPE BERCHESI

69

CONVERSIONS

20   RICHIE MO'UNGA

14   ELTON JANTJIES

11   OWEN FARRELL

10   DAN BIGGAR

9   HANDRE POLLARD

CARDS ISSUED

There were a record amount of red cards issued during the tournament, eight in total. A further twenty eight yellow cards were issued as well.

RED CARDS

John Quill	USA vs ENGLAND
Facundo Gattas	URUGUAY vs GEORGIA
Ed Fidow	SAMOA vs SCOTLAND
Andrea Lovotti	ITALY vs SOUTH AFRICA
Tomas Lavinini	ARGENTINA vs ENGLAND
Josh Larsen	CANADA vs SOUTH AFRICA
Bundee Aki	IRELAND vs SAMOA
Sebastien Vahaamahina	FRANCE vs WALES

YELLOW CARDS

Levani Botia	FIJI vs AUSTRALIA
Tadhg Berne	IRELAND vs SCOTLAND
Jaba Bregvadze	GEORGIA vs WALES
Kirill Gotovsev	RUSSIA vs SAMOA
Motu Matu'u	SAMOA vs RUSSIA
Ray Lee Lo	SAMOA vs RUSIA
Matt Heaton	CANADA vs ITALY
Adriaan Booysen	NAMIBIA vs SOUTH AFRICA
Johan Coetsee	NAMIBIA vs SOUTH AFRICA
Ed Fidow	SAMOA vs SCOTLAND
Bogden Fedolko	RUSSIA vs IRELAND
Andrey Oshkov	RUSSIA vs IRELAND
Adam Coleman	AUSTRALIA vs URUGUAY
Lukhan Salakaia	AUSTRALIA vs URUGUAY

TJ Ioane	SAMOA vs JAPAN
Nepo Laulala	NEW ZEALAND vs NAMIBIA
Ofa Tuungafasi	NEW ZEALAND vs NAMIBIA
Ken Owens	WALES vs FIJI
James Davies	WALES vs FIJI
Tevita Cavubati	FIJI vs WALES
Semi Kunatani	FIJI vs WALES
Isi Naisarani	AUSTRALIA vs GEORGIA
Seilala Lam	SAMOA vs IRELAND
TJ Ioane	SAMOA vs IRELAND
Santiago Civetta	URUGUAY vs WALES
Matt Todd	NEW ZEALAND vs IRELAND
Ross Moriarty	WALES vs SCOTLAND
Tendai Mtawarira	SOUTH AFRICA vs JAPAN

THE HOST NATION

Japan upset the Springboks at the 2015 tournament, winning 34 – 32. They managed to score two more wins in the poll stage but failed to qualify for the quarter finals. They aimed to do even better in the 2019 event and managed qualify for the quarter finals for the first time in their history.

They started the tournament against Russia in the opening match. They won by 30 – 10 with winger Kotaro Matsushima scoring a hat trick. Next up was the Irish team that entered the tournament as the number one ranked side in the world, largely due to their 2018 exploits.

Japan shocked Ireland by winning 19 – 12 after the Irish had scored first and looked dangerous in the opening minutes. But the Japanese team took control of the match and deserved their win.

Their third pool match was against Samoa and they won the match by 38 – 19. The final pool match against Scotland was in the balance as it

looked like it would have to be cancelled due to Typhoon Hagibis. The match however went ahead and the Japanese won by 28 – 21, topping their pool after an unbeaten run through their pool matches.

Their quarter final opponents were to be South Africa. Two weeks before the tournament started the South Africans beat them comprehensively by 41 – 7. This was however knockout rugby and the team had the backing of just about every other nation apart from South Africa as they headed into the match.

Makazole Mapimpi score a try early for South Africa but the South Africans struggled to get momentum and at half time they held a slender lead of 5 – 3.

However they managed to dominate the second half and win by the match by 26 – 3. But the Japanese team could hold their heads high as they were worthy of their place among the top eight teams. The inspired leadership of captain Michael Leitch, coupled with the shrewd coaching of former All Black Jamie Joseph, helped the team to not only compete at this level but to excel whilst doing so.

The Japanese people were excellent hosts as they took to supporting the other teams once Japan as knocked out. In the aftermath there were calls for them to be included in the Rugby Championship or the Six Nations. Their inclusion seems to be imminent at the time of writing.

It is indeed imperative that they be included in either of these tournaments as soon as possible. They would be an asset to either and both of the afore mentioned tournaments could do with a shake up.

OVERALL WORLD CUP WINNERS

1987   NEW ZEALAND

1991   AUSTRALIA

1995   SOUTH AFRICA

1999   AUSTRALIA

2003   ENGLAND

2007   SOUTH AFRICA

2011   NEW ZEALAND

2015   NEW ZEALAND

2019   SOUTH AFRICA

TEAM BY TEAM RESULTS

ARGENTINA

France	Lost 21 – 23
Tonga	Won 28 – 12
England	Lost 10 – 39
USA	Won 47 – 17

A narrow loss against France in their opening match made the test against England a must win. That match was lost and thus Argentina failed to progress beyond the pool stage, although it should be noted that they were in a tough pool and there was always going to be a major team from the pool that would not progress.

Argentina will be motivated to do better in the next tournament in 2023.

AUSTRALIA

Fiji   Won 39 – 21

Wales   Lost 25 – 29

Uruguay   Won 45 – 10

Georgia   Won 27 – 8

England   Lost 16 – 40

Their crunch match against Wales was lost and that put them on a collision course with an in form English side. They never really got going and lost the quarter final against England by a wide margin.

During the tournament they showed brief glimpses of what they are capable of but they were never able to sustain that. The two time champions will be hurting and with coach Michael Cheika stepping down it is a good time for them to rebuild.

CANADA

Italy   Lost 7 – 48

New Zealand Lost 0 – 63

South Africa   Lost 7 – 66

Namibia   Cancelled

Having lost heavily against Italy, South Africa and New Zealand the Canadians would have targeted the Namibians in their final pool match. Unfortunately Typhoon Hagibis intervened and the match was called off.

ENGLAND

Tonga	Won 35 – 3
USA	Won 45 – 7
Argentina	Won 39 – 10
France	Cancelled
Australia	Won 40 – 16
New Zealand	Won 19 – 7
South Africa	Lost 12 – 32

England breezed through their pool matches and coach Eddie Jones was more than happy to take a draw from the cancelled pool match against France. The Australians were smashed in the quarter final and set up a semi against New Zealand.

With few observers outside England giving them much of a chance they surprised in just how much they dominated the All Blacks in that semi final. The Kiwis were simply not able to get going and it took England just two minutes to score a try through Manu Tuilagi. Rarely has the All Blacks looked so overwhelmed and the match was won by 19 – 7.

And so England marched on to the final and were indeed the favourites to win their second title, their first being the 2003 victory. England seemed to make the same mistake the kiwis made with them as they appeared to underestimate the South Africans in the lead up to the final.

After just two minutes it was clear to see that England would not have things all their own way and as the match wore on the South Africans took complete control of the match.

Kyle Sinckler and Maro Itoje courted some controversy as they refused to wear their silver medals after the match. England can however hold their heads up high as they have a core of excellent young players that bodes well for their future.

Young flankers Tom Curry and Sam Underhill comes to mind and both of them have big careers ahead of them. Add to that the likes of Itoje and Watson and it is clear that England will present a tough challenge come France in 2023.

FIJI

Australia	Lost 21 – 39
Uruguay	Lost 27 – 30
Georgia	Won 45 – 10
Wales	Lost 17 – 29

Fiji troubled Australia for large parts of their opening match and would have fancied their chances against Uruguay. They managed to score five tries in that match but only managed to convert one of them, at the same time Berchesi had his kicking boots on and helped Uruguay produce an upset in winning the match 30 – 27.

They beat Georgia but were unable to upset the Welsh team and so they failed to progress beyond the pool stage.

FRANCE

Argentina	Won 23 – 21
USA	Won 33 – 9
Tonga	Won 23 – 21
England	Cancelled
Wales	Lost 19 – 20

The French went through the pool stage unbeaten, aided by the cancelled match against England. They almost came unstuck against the Tongans and going into the quarter final it was anybody's guess as to what French team would show up on the day.

They dominated the match and was leading by 19 – 13 when Sebastien Vahaamahina hit Aaron Wainwright with his elbow in the face. He was subsequently red carded and Wales was able to score the try to win by a single point. Vahaamahina duly announced his retirement from test rugby.

GEORGIA

Wales   Lost 14 – 43

Uruguay   Won 33 – 7

Fiji   Lost 10 – 45

Australia Lost 8 - 27

The Georgians would really only have one realistic chance at winning a test and that was the Uruguay match. They managed to do just that and made the Australians work hard for their victory in the final pool match.

IRELAND

Scotland	Won 27 – 3
Japan	Lost 12 – 19
Russia	Won 35 – 0
Samoa	Won 47 – 5
New Zealand	Lost 14 - 46

Ireland had a banner year in 2018 and seemed poised to make a big impact at the 2019 event. Their form in 2019 however showed that they had peeked a year too early. After their opening win against the Scots they seemed back on track but the loss against Japan derailed their campaign.

They were completely outplayed by the All Blacks in the quarter final and once again failed to progress past that stage. Long serving captain Rory Best retired after that match and coach Joe Schmidt has moved on as well. Best played in 124 test matches.

ITALY

Namibia	Won 47 – 22
Canada	Won 48 – 7
South Africa	Lost 3 – 49
New Zealand	Cancelled

Having won their first two matches they were looking to upset the Boks but lost comprehensively. Their final pool match was them cancelled and sadly that meant that three of their centurions retired on a training pitch and not after playing the All Blacks.

Captain Sergio Parisse (142) , Leonardo Ghiraldini (104) and Alessandro Zanni (115) bid farewell in a most unsatisfying way.

JAPAN

Russia	Won 30 – 10
Ireland	Won 19 – 12
Samoa	Won 38 – 19
Scotland	Won 28 – 21
South Africa	Lost 3 - 26

An unbeaten run through their pool set up a quarter final against the South Africans. Having shocked the Ireland and Scotland teams they were simply unable to match the physicality of the Boks. Nevertheless they made their mark and won many admirers for their style of play.

NAMIBIA

Italy	Lost 22 – 47
South Africa	Lost 3 – 57
New Zealand	Lost 9 – 71
Canada	Cancelled

After a strong performance against Italy they were pulverised by the Boks and the All Blacks. They would still have fancied a go at the Canadians in the final pool match but unfortunately that match fell victim to the Typhoon Hagibis.

NEW ZEALAND

South Africa	Won 23 – 13
Canada	Won 63 – 0
Namibia	Won 71 – 9
Italy	Cancelled
Ireland	Won 46 – 14
England	Lost 7 - 19
Wales	Won 40 – 17

The defending champions were looking to add a fourth overall title as well as a third in a row. They were overwhelming favourites and were able to beat the Boks in the opening pool match.

From there they went on to smash the Canadians as well as the Namibians. Their final pool match was cancelled and they managed to top their pool. The Ireland team was up next in the quarter final and the All Blacks left nothing to chance as they won the match by 46 – 14. That set up a semi final against England and again they were seen as the favourites heading into that match. It is hard to recall a match where the Kiwis were so dominated as the English were simply awesome in winning by 19 – 7.

Even the try scored by Ardie Savea was gifted to them and at no other stage did they look like scoring, and that is simply not something to be expected from them.

They were doomed to play the third place play off match, or bronze final as it is now called. Wales were to be their opponents and although the All Blacks would probably have preferred playing in the final the next day they managed to find their form again and won by 40 – 17.

It was a fitting send off to their coach Steve Hansen who had guided them to 93 wins in a total of 107 tests as coach.

They also said farewell to captain Kieran Read (127) , Sonny Bill Williams (58), Ben Smith (84) and Ryan Crotty (48).

No doubt the Kiwis will be hurting but there is also no doubt they will be back and looking to win the title again come 2023.

RUSSIA

Japan   Lost 10 – 30

Samoa   Lost 9 – 34

Ireland   Lost 0 – 35

Scotland Lost 0 – 61

The Russians were up against it and were unable to win any of their matches during the pool stage.

SAMOA

Russia	Won 34 – 9
Scotland	Lost 0 – 34
Japan	Lost 19 – 38
Ireland	Lost 5 – 47

Samoa is always capable of causing an upset but they were unable to do so this time around. Their poor discipline cost them again and apart from their win in the opening game against Russia they were unable to win any further matches. At the same time it is imperative that the island nations are taken care of and it appears that Samoan rugby has gone backwards quite alarmingly.

SCOTLAND

Ireland	Lost 3 – 27
Samoa	Won 34 – 9
Russia	Won 61 – 9
Japan	Lost 21 – 28

The Scots were on the back foot as soon as the Irish beat them so comprehensively I the opening match. They won their next two matches to give themselves a chance but they succumbed to the Japanese team in their final pool match.

The team was unable to progress beyond the pool stage and no doubt they will be looking for answers before the next tournament.

SOUTH AFRICA

New Zealand	Lost 13 – 23
Namibia	Won 57 – 3
Italy	Won 49 – 3
Canada	Won 66 – 7
Japan	Won 26 – 3
Wales	Won 19 – 16
England	Won 32 – 12

After their loss in the opening match against the Kiwis nobody was giving the Boks much of a chance of winning the tournament. They won the rest of their pool matches by wide margins and met the Japanese in the quarter finals.

They brought the Japanese fairy tale to a sudden halt when they won the match by 26 – 3. Their performance in the semi final against Wales was however probably their poorest of the year as they managed to scrape through by 19 – 16, largely thanks to a solo try by Damian de Allende. As the final against England came closer the English were seen as the overwhelming favourites after they dismantled the All Blacks. However the Springboks managed to find several extra gears as they dominated the English from the outset in every facet of play. They were leading by 18 – 12 when they scored the first of two tries to ultimately win by 32 - 12 .

It was their third title and the two tries scored were their first tries scored in a final. They have now played three finals and won all three. Handre Pollard was the top points scorer in the tournament with 69 and Makazole Mapimpi ended up with six tries, one behind top try scorer Josh Adams of Wales.

After the tournament their prop Tendai Matawarira, known as Beast, announced his retirement after playing in 117 test matches. He had made his debut back in 2008.

Francois Louw also retired after playing 76 tests and earlier in the tournament Schalk Brits also retired after 15 tests. The day after the final the team were crowned team of the year, their coach won the coach of the year award and finally Pieter Steph du Toit won the World player of the year award.

TONGA

England	Lost 3 – 35
Argentina	Lost 12 – 28
France	Lost 21 – 23
USA	Won 31 – 19

The Tongans found themselves in a very tough pool , but despite the fact that they lost their first two matches they came within two points of causing an upset against France.

They finished off on a winning note when the beat the United States by 31 – 19.

URUGUAY

Fiji   Won 30 – 27

Georgia   Lost 7 - 33

Australia   Lost 10 – 45

Wales   Lost 13 – 35

After their shock win against Fiji in their opening match they would have seen their next match against Georgia as a possible win. But the Georgians brought them back to earth and from there they lost both their last two matches in the pool stage.

UNITED STATES

England	Lost 7 – 45
France	Lost 9 – 33
Argentina	Lost 17 – 47
Tonga	Lost 19 – 31

The Americans found themselves in a tough pool and their only chance at winning a match would have been the Tongan match up. They however lost that match and thus failed to win any of their pool matches.

WALES

Georgia	Won 43 – 14
Australia	Won 29 – 25
Fiji	Won 29 – 17
Uruguay	Won 35 – 13
France	Won 20 – 19
South Africa	Lost 16 – 19
New Zealand	Lost 17 - 40

Wales topped their pool but were the recipients of a healthy dose of luck against the French as they lost Vahaamahina to a red card. Even then the Welsh struggled to push on but managed to score a try and win by 20 – 19.

The semi final against South Africa was an ugly match as neither team seemed to be in the mood to play much rugby. The Welsh lost and played the Kiwis in the bronze final, a test they lost by 17 – 40.

On the plus side young winger Josh Adams ended up as the top try scorer of the tournament with 7 tries.

THE 2023 WORLD CUP

The 2023 edition is scheduled to kick off on the 8th of September 2023 in France.

Thank you for reading and see you in France !

DEDICATION

This book is dedicated to Johan van Loggerenberg, known as Loggies to his many friends. He was my uncle but so much more than that. He took me to my first rugby match back in 1982 as the famous Ellis Park was re opened and in 1984 he took me to my first test match at the same venue as South Africa beat England 35 – 9 and Danie Gerber scored a hat trick. As I became an adult our outings to Ellis Park became less frequent but his son Renier was there to fill the gap and together they spent many a day at Ellis Park cheering on their team.

In 2010 we attended the historic match at Soweto between South Africa and New Zealand, a crowd of 92 000 was a sight to behold. In 2012 the English again clashed with the Boks at Ellis Park and I was fortunate to attend with them. Once again, bringing us full circle.

Loggies himself played well over a 100 matches at prop for Edenvale and as time marched on he was part of the Tendella Golden Oldies team.

He is sorely missed. He is survived by his wife Dawn, son Renier and daughter Bianca.

108

JOHAN VAN LOGGERENBERG

11 AUGUST 1959 – 8 JUNE 2018

REST IN PEACE

Loggies pictured before the NZ/SA match in Soweto in 2010.

This is book is an unofficial review of the World Cup in 2019. It is purely from a fan's perspective and not meant to be seen as an official review.

Also by Wayne Grobler :

Line of Fire : Blood, Sweat and Tears in the South African Police.

Printed in Poland
by Amazon Fulfillment
Poland Sp. z o.o., Wrocław